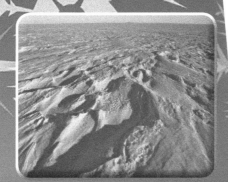

SOUTHERN OCEAN

ANTARCTICA

Blizzard, so had to keep digging the tent out of the snow

You got there!

Mt Erebus: Southernmost active volcano

Astrolabe Basin: World's thickest ice – 4776 m deep

ir

er	ur	ir

Read the words.

Set 1 (13 words)	Set 2 (20 words)	Set 3 (20 words)	Set 4 (20 words)	Set 5 (20 words)
thirteenth	firm	confirm	shirty	hummingbird
birthday	thirst	girlfriend	squirting	circumstance
Shirley	birth	thirteen	firstly	unconfirmed
circus	stir	affirm	circles	dirtiest
skirt	squirm	sirloin	firmness	thirstiest
shirt	whirl	virtue	chirpy	virtuous
circle	chirp	birdsong	confirmed	stirringly
whirling	Sir	birthmark	birches	circumvent
twirling	birch	whirlpool	squirming	flirtation
first	squirt	swirling	firmest	reconfirm
third	smirk	thirdly	circling	encircled
bird	fir	dirty	thirtieth	virtually
dirt	flirt	thirty	virtual	semicircle
13 words so far	swirl	quirky	dirtier	confirmation
	firms	irksome	circular	circulation
	shirk	thirsty	thirstier	circulating
	quirk	stirring	circulate	infirmary
	mirth	whirlwind	thirstiness	infirmaries
	girth	birthdays	circuses	virtuously
	smirked	firmly	shirtily	circumnavigation
	33 words so far	53 words so far	73 words so far	93 words so far

	up to 39 Sparking	40–49 Glowing	50–59 Burning	60–69 Sizzling	70+ Red hot!
Score/Date					
Score/Date					

One Minute Wonders

4

Read the story then draw the picture.

For her thirteenth birthday, Shirley went to the circus in her brand new skirt and shirt. She sat next to the circle and watched the acrobats whirling and twirling above her. At first, all went well, but in the third act a bird flew in and dropped dirt on Shirley's skirt! Oh dear!

Practise writing.

Build your word power.

Well done!
ui
oo
Silent Letters
ea
ow
ou
aw
au
oy
oi
ir

Brilliant! You are off!

Firstly, you have found a team with all the qualities needed: fitness, bravery, loyalty, respect, pride, attention to detail and leadership. No one can shirk their share of the work. Antarctica is a very dangerous place. Circumstances can change at any moment and there is no rescue service, so having the right people with you is a matter of life and death.

oi

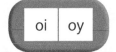

| oi | oy |

Read the words.

Set 1 (11 words)	Set 2 (20 words)	Set 3 (20 words)	Set 4 (20 words)	Set 5 (20 words)
avoid	**point**	foiled	noisy	rejoicing
poisonous	**voice**	moisture	boiler	appointment
toilet	**join**	poison	oily	noisiest
choice	**appoint**	anoint	coiling	exploited
moist	noise	embroil	moistened	loitering
soil	coin	poignant	voiceless	exploiting
boiling	spoil	ointment	spoilsport	humanoid
oil	joint	recoil	oilier	moisturise
coiled	boil	rejoice	noisier	pointlessly
noises	toil	exploit	adjoining	joinery
loiter	joist	android	disjointed	noiselessly
11 words so far	groin	steroid	pointedly	moisturising
	foil	moisten	embroider	embroidery
	hoist	voices	recoiling	exploitation
	void	spoiling	disappoint	disappointing
	oink	uncoil	boisterous	embroidering
	poise	unspoiled	noisily	boisterously
	spoilt	embroiled	avoiding	disappointment
	foist	jointed	anointed	disappointed
	poised	pointless	noisiness	unavoidable
	31 words so far	51 words so far	71 words so far	91 words so far

	up to 39 Sparking	**40–49** Glowing	**50–59** Burning	**60–69** Sizzling	**70+** Red hot!
Score/Date					
Score/Date					

One Minute Wonders

6

Read the story then draw the picture.

Avoid the poisonous toilet if you have the choice. It's full of moist soil, boiling oil and coiled snakes! It is making truly terrible noises. Don't loiter …

Practise writing.

Build your word power.

Well done!
ui
oo
Silent Letters
ea
ow
ou
aw
au
oy
oi
ir

Brilliant! You made it to the next stage!

It is summer in the Southern Hemisphere and the best time to go. You have landed safely on Antarctica in a noisy Hercules, specially fitted with skis. The ice can be 4 kilometres deep! Your aim is the geographical South Pole, one of the most remote, extreme and untouched places on earth; it is an incredible, breathtaking landscape. You have made a good choice of campsite for the first night and all your equipment is unpacked.

oy

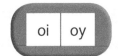

oi | oy

Destroy the Convoy!

By Charles

Read the words.

Set 1 (11 words)	Set 2 (17 words)	Set 3 (18 words)	Set 4 (18 words)	Set 5 (18 words)
joyfully	**employ**	decoy	soya	annoyance
boy	**enjoy**	boyish	cowboy	employee
toy	joy	destroyed	oyster	employer
enjoyed	ploy	deployed	soybean	loyally
voyage	buoy	buoyant	employment	disloyal
employed	coy	tomboy	annoying	loyalty
loyal	groyne	joyless	employing	royalist
royal	buoys	killjoy	enjoyment	royalty
annoyed	boys	toyshop	destroyer	clairvoyant
destroy	toys	joystick	buoyancy	royalties
convoy	annoy	annoys	joyrider	disloyalty
11 words so far	ahoy	enjoys	destroying	redeployment
	alloy	viceroy	redeploy	employable
	envoy	coyly	overjoyed	enjoyable
	deploy	cloying	flamboyant	boysenberry
	joyful	gargoyle	joyriding	oystercatcher
	boycott	foyer	boycotted	boysenberries
	28 words so far	alloys	deployment	flamboyantly
		46 words so far	64 words so far	82 words so far

One Minute Wonders

	up to 39 Sparking	40–49 Glowing	50–59 Burning	60–69 Sizzling	70+ Red hot!
Score/Date					
Score/Date					

8

Read the story then draw the picture.

Joyfully, the boy played with his toy ships. He enjoyed taking them on a voyage around the bath. He employed a loyal captain for the royal ship at the front. But suddenly, he became annoyed with the game. "Destroy the convoy!" he cried and sank them all.

Practise writing.

Build your word power.

Brilliant! You made it to the next stage!

You are up and dressed for your first day of skiing, feeling buoyant. The weather in Antarctica is the harshest in the world. Temperatures have once plummeted as low as −89.2°C and winds can be up to 193 kilometres per hour in summer, more in winter. You have three layers of clothes for your legs and five on the top. There are three layers on your head and hands and, after that, sunglasses and goggles. If your skin is exposed to the cold you will get frostbite, which could destroy any hopes of achieving your goal.

au

or | au | augh

My Naughty Daughter

By Patricia

Read the words.

Set 1 (11 words)	Set 2 (20 words)	Set 3 (20 words)	Set 4 (20 words)	Set 5 (20 words)
autumn	**cause**	saucer	slaughtered	haughtily
naughty	pause	cauldron	hauling	gaudily
daughter	launch	jaunty	taunted	sauntering
haunted	clause	assault	launches	fraudulent
sauce	vault	saunter	daunting	applauding
caught	gaunt	cautious	authors	exhausting
caution	daub	auburn	haunting	naughtier
fault	faun	exhaust	launderette	precaution
exhausted	Paul	author	audible	gaudier
laundry	gauze	haughty	authentic	naughtiest
taught	maul	caustic	cautiously	applauded
	haul	gaudy	autumnal	auditory
	taunt	austere	nautical	cautionary
	haunch	slaughter	astronaut	exhaustedly
	hauled	applaud	dinosaur	auditioning
	daubed	August	audience	automatic
	mauled	sauna	plausible	authority
	caused	saucy	audition	auditorium
	paused	applause	overhaul	tyrannosaurus
	launched	pausing	assaulted	automatically
11 words so far	31 words so far	51 words so far	71 words so far	91 words so far

One Minute Wonders

	up to 39 Sparking	40–49 Glowing	50–59 Burning	60–69 Sizzling	70+ Red hot!
Score/Date					
Score/Date					

10

Read the story then draw the picture.

Last autumn, my naughty daughter pretended that our house was haunted by covering herself in a sheet with tomato sauce on top. When I caught her, I gave her a caution, saying, "It's your fault we are all exhausted. As a punishment, you can do all the laundry this week."

I think that taught her a lesson.

Practise writing.

Build your word power.

Brilliant! You made it to the next stage!

4

You did months of training, hauling the 115 kilogram pulk, using tyres strapped together, and pulling them along roads. The muscles in your legs and back are now very strong. Without supreme fitness, exhaustion could set in and lead to injuries. You have been taught that this is extremely dangerous in such harsh conditions. You cannot be too cautious. Suddenly, a blizzard of ice crystals is whipped up by the wind; they are so fine that they get between the slits of your closed eyes. You hunker down until it is over.

Sizzling Syllables! (1)

Read the syllables.

Six syllable types

Closed	isk	ank	ift	ost	ump	ind	amp	ilt	ot	ulf
Open	sta	ve	quo	pru	thi	jo	ni	da	ste	to
Evil e	obe	epe	ike	ice	ube	age	ele	ipe	one	uge
Vowel	moi	hea	foo	roy	nau	mow	few	snai	sau	lay
-r	tar	mer	tor	mar	per	bor	arb	ger	ord	nar
-le	-fle	-dle	-tle	-ple	-cle	-ble	-sle	-kle	-gle	-zle

Got it? ☐

Ski the South Pole patterns

irst	oil	voy	aul	oilt	lau	fir
loy	shir	oin	aut	irt	ploi	noy
oid	sau	irm	voi	gau	irl	aug
troy	irth	broi	cau	ploy	plau	oice

Got it? ☐

Prefixes and suffixes

super-	-like	-dom	en-	ex-	-ward	ir-
ambi-	il-	auto	ante	extra-	out-	trans-
contra-	-ish	-ability	-hood	-ship	post-	-some

Got it? ☐

12

Fiery Phrases!

Birthday Girl	Poisonous Toilet	Destroy the Convoy!	My Naughty Daughter

Read the phrases.

Set 1	Set 2	Set 3
a beautiful new skirt	avoid the puddle	pause for a moment
his fourth birthday	the boisterous puppy	the author of the book
two birds flew higher	an android tablet	pass the sauce, please
the chick chirped loudly	loitering at the corner	the audience applauded
it went round in a circle	dentist appointment	caused an accident
the fir tree on the hill	poised to leap	mauled by a lion
the circus came to town	moisture in the air	a daunting task
take the third turning	very annoying	driving cautiously
he shook hands firmly	a disloyal friend	audition for the play
the runner was very thirsty	the royal family	gaudy decorations
the cook stirred the stew	jumping for joy	applaud the winner
tickling makes you squirm	a long voyage	the sound was audible
thirty days in November	what a killjoy	the naughty kitten
look at the whirlpool	in the foyer of the cinema	haul on the rope
your holiday is confirmed	the building was destroyed	sauntering down the road
is there a choice	he was overjoyed	lying in the sauna
what is the point	toying with the idea	at the launderette
coiling the rope	taking the joystick	an automatic car
a great disappointment	deploy the troops	he's exhausted
what a noise	launch a rocket	I caught a cold
20 phrases	20 phrases	20 phrases

	up to 29 Sparking	30–39 Glowing	40–49 Burning	50–59 Sizzling	60+ Red hot!
Score/Date					
Score/Date					

One Minute Wonders

aw

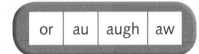

or | au | augh | aw

Awful Hawk

By Matthew

Read the words.

Set 1 (9 words)	Set 2 (19 words)	Set 3 (19 words)	Set 4 (19 words)	Set 5 (19 words)
dawn	**law**	gawp	in-laws	sawing
squawk	awkward	spawn	withdraw	squawking
saw	crawl	claw	lawyers	gawping
awful	raw	sawn	dawdled	jigsaws
hawk	thaw	yawned	hawthorn	awning
draw	drawn	squawked	flawless	trawlers
claws	prawn	hawks	redraw	awesome
straw	lawn	sprawl	outlawed	awestruck
jaws	shawl	dawned	lawful	awnings
9 words so far	yawn	gnawed	brawny	awkwardly
	gnaw	crawled	thawing	awfully
	awe	sprawled	withdrawn	unlawful
	jaw	jigsaw	scrawny	strawberry
	brawl	tawny	dawdling	scrawnier
	scrawl	lawyer	gnawing	flawlessly
	pawn	pawpaw	dawning	scrawniest
	drawer	trawler	drawing	strawberries
	flaw	jackdaw	sprawling	awkwardness
	paws	dawdle	yawning	unlawfully
	28 words so far	47 words so far	66 words so far	85 words so far

One Minute Wonders

	up to 39 Sparking	40–49 Glowing	50–59 Burning	60–69 Sizzling	70+ Red hot!
Score/Date					
Score/Date					

14

Read the story then draw the picture.

At dawn, the baby rabbit gave a squawk as it saw the awful hawk. Its mother flew over to draw the hawk away while the baby dug quickly with its claws to hide in the straw. It was saved from the jaws of death.

Practise writing.

Build your word power.

Well done!
ui
oo
Silent Letters
ea
ow
ou
aw
au
oy
oi
ir

Brilliant! You made it to the next stage!

5

It was your turn to be leader and you have just completed your first hour and a half of walking. You can take a five-minute rest, but you cannot dawdle or you will freeze. After all, even moderate hypothermia results in violent shivering, laborious walking, loss of balance and an inability to make the right decisions. Also you must make sure you drink enough of the water that you get from melting the snow; you need to drink about four litres a day. The enormous expanse of dazzling snow fills you with awe.

Loud Mouse

By Tom

ou	ow

Read the words.

Set 1 (11 words)	**Set 2** (20 words)	**Set 3** (20 words)	**Set 4** (20 words)	**Set 5** (20 words)
loud	**our**	flour	aloud	loudness
mouse	**out**	spout	account	fountain
shouting	**found**	blouse	counter	boundless
about	**ground**	bound	county	founded
house	**south**	joust	flounder	miscount
hour	**round**	sprout	lousy	voucher
underground	**count**	gouge	counsel	pronounce
sound	**cloud**	lounge	bounty	devoured
pounce	**mouth**	mound	compound	bouncing
announced	**proud**	couch	checkout	confound
outraged	**pounds**	bounce	doubtless	outwitted
11 words so far	**shout**	hound	founder	foundation
	doubt	bout	devout	boundary
	ounce	foul	pronoun	encounter
	outside	clout	surround	astounded
	thousands	drought	discount	outrageous
	amount	flounce	devour	announcement
	mountain	grouch	outrage	floundering
	council	crouch	outlaw	councillor
	around	flounced	bouncy	unpronounceable
	31 words so far	51 words so far	71 words so far	91 words so far

One Minute Wonders

	up to 39 Sparking	**40–49** Glowing	**50–59** Burning	**60–69** Sizzling	**70+** Red hot!
Score/Date					
Score/Date					

16

Read the story then draw the picture.

"Oh! You loud mouse! Stop shouting all about the house at this hour. Stay underground and don't make a sound or I'll pounce!" announced the outraged cat.

Practise writing.

Build your word power.

Brilliant! You made it to the next stage!

Well done!
ui
oo
Silent Letters
ea
ow
ou
aw
au
oy
oi
ir

You are doing brilliantly. The total expedition is almost 1000 kilometres to the South Pole. For the first ten days, you have been covering 12 kilometres a day so you have now completed 120 kilometres. For the next ten days, you will be doing 20 kilometres a day and after that, 25 kilometres a day. You have the compass bound to your arm so you don't have to stop and get it out of your pocket to check you are going the correct way. Every three hours you will check the GPS, so there will be no doubt that you are in the right place.

OW

Not Now Brown Cow!

By Valentine

Read the words.

Set 1 (11 words)	Set 2 (15 words)	Set 3 (16 words)	Set 4 (16 words)
wow	**how**	chow	glowered
crowd	**allow**	browse	crowded
town	**power**	frowned	cowered
row	**flower**	coward	powdered
down	**however**	shower	flowered
frowned	frown	brownie	flowering
howled	owl	dowry	cowardly
allowed	growl	cower	powering
now	clown	glower	powerful
brown	drown	endow	allowance
cow	fowl	chowder	glowering
11 words so far	vow	powder	endowment
	gown	dowdy	cowardice
	brow	powwow	powerfully
	bow	drowning	non-flowering
	26 words so far	browsing	overpowering
		42 words so far	58 words so far

One Minute Wonders

	up to 39 Sparking	40–49 Glowing	50–59 Burning	60–69 Sizzling	70+ Red hot!
Score/Date					
Score/Date					

Read the story then draw the picture.

Wow! What a crowd in town! What a row! I looked down. I frowned and howled, "It should not be allowed. Not now brown cow!"

Practise writing.

Build your word power.

Brilliant! You made it to the next stage!

There was a howling blizzard last night and the winds reached almost 200 kilometres per hour. The powdery snow was drifting and was beginning to drown the tents. You had to get up every two hours to dig it away, otherwise you would have been buried and may have died of suffocation. However, all is well now. You wrap up your wrists, ankles and neck as they can soon become very cold and uncomfortable. They can lose a lot of heat quickly as they pass the blood between other well-insulated areas.

Bread Head

By Nico

Read the words.

Set 1 (12 words)	Set 2 (20 words)	Set 3 (20 words)	Set 4 (20 words)	Set 5 (20 words)
bread	**read**	threats	deafen	heavily
head	**dead**	sweat	abreast	treachery
heaven	**lead**	deadly	breathless	steadier
weather	**spread**	feather	treasured	jealousy
dreadfully	**breadth**	pleasure	measured	stealthier
sweating	**health**	steady	weapons	measuring
already	**ahead**	jealous	treading	wealthier
treasure	**measure**	forehead	deathly	leathery
leather	**ready**	weapon	spreading	treasuring
meadow	**heavy**	sweater	unread	steadiest
wealthy	**instead**	pleasant	sweaters	pleasantly
breathlessly	breath	treading	pheasants	treacherous
12 words so far	tread	leaden	feathers	unpleasant
	meant	threadbare	misread	heaviest
	threat	breakfast	unsteady	heavenly
	deaf	pheasant	steadily	wealthiest
	dread	healthy	heavier	threateningly
	death	threaten	jealously	unsteadily
	breast	dreadful	threatening	unpleasantly
	thread	threaded	readily	treacherously
	32 words so far	52 words so far	72 words so far	92 words so far

	up to 39 Sparking	40–49 Glowing	50–59 Burning	60–69 Sizzling	70+ Red hot!
Score/Date					
Score/Date					

One Minute Wonders

Read the story then draw the picture.

Bread Head was in heaven! The weather was dreadfully hot and he was sweating profusely. However, he had already found the treasure. It had been hidden under a rock in a leather box near the gate into the meadow.

"I will be wealthy!" he exclaimed breathlessly.

Practise writing.

Build your word power.

Brilliant! You made it to the next stage!

8

In summer in the Southern Hemisphere the sun never sets, so it is daylight all through the night. It is dreadfully difficult to relax and sleep at night because of the danger you are in. Four and a half hours is the most you are likely to get, which is not pleasant! You are thankful that you have your three pairs of gloves to wear: a light first layer, then an insulating layer and a weatherproof outer layer. You are reaching the Polar Plateau, where there is the threat of altitude sickness, so you must stop to rest if you feel unwell.

Well done!
ui
oo
Silent Letters
ea
ow
ou
aw
au
oy
oi
ir

Sizzling Syllables! ②

Read the syllables.

Cycle Africa **review**

kit	gy	bur	odge	cend	tur	oes
ous	kin	guil	cept	gen	ture	gues
cel	thur	ket	gi	ous	tion	edge
ges	kip	tion	ture	gui	ceed	ives

Got it? ☐

New *Ski the South Pole* **patterns**

paw	oud	hea	owd	ead	sou	scraw
pow	mea	gaw	lou	rea	how	eav
plea	draw	grou	eath	dow	haw	ount
straw	brow	owl	saw	ound	frow	thou

Got it? ☐

All *Ski the South Pole* **so far**

auth	poi	flaw	foy	clow	irk	oit
oul	hoy	whir	eav	plau	flou	coy
flir	brow	aud	traw	cir	choi	phea
eap	awp	ird	ouch	joy	drow	aut

Got it? ☐

Fiery Phrases! ②

Awful Hawk	Loud Mouse	Not Now Brown Cow!	Bread Head

Read the phrases.

Set 1	Set 2	Set 3
yawning loudly	a cloudy sky	browsing through the books
sprawled on the sofa	bank account	have a shower
an awesome sight	boundless energy	the rose is flowering
lying in the straw	a proud moment	make an allowance
strawberries and cream	bouncy castle	take a bow
put it in the drawer	what is the amount	tread carefully
the parrot squawked	reading aloud	straight ahead
the huge jigsaw	puzzle at the checkout	what's for breakfast
an awkward moment	a beautiful fountain	what dreadful weather
against the law	two discount vouchers	ran out of breath
the ice thawed	the girl flounced out	the treasure hunt
eat some raw vegetables	you are not allowed	light as a feather
the day dawned	the grumpy man frowned	hold it steadily
gnawing on the bone	a powerful swimmer	spread the butter
brother-in-law	he was a coward	a leather belt
it was awful	the dog growled	finished already
dawdling along	excellent washing powder	heavier than ever
wrapped in a shawl	the queen's crown	in good health
round and about	a crowded room	don't be jealous
thousands of pounds	chocolate brownies	a beautiful pheasant
20 phrases	20 phrases	20 phrases

	up to 29 Sparking	30–39 Glowing	40–49 Burning	50–59 Sizzling	60+ Red hot!
Score/Date					
Score/Date					

One Minute Wonders

Sneaky Silent Letters

w h l

White Whale

By Harry

Read the words.

Wriggling Wren		White Whale		Talking Calf
Set 1 (15 words)	**Set 2** (19 words)	**Set 3** (19 words)	**Set 4** (19 words)	**Set 5** (19 words)
wreck	**written**	**white**	whip	**walk**
whole	wrench	whale	wheeze	**talk**
wrapped	wrap	**whizzed**	whiff	**would**
answered	sword	**where**	whacked	**should**
who	wrath	**when**	whine	**could**
write	wreath	exhausted	whirl	**half**
whose	writhe	honour	wheat	calm
answer	wrung	**what**	whack	palm
two	wrecked	**why**	whisky	psalm
wrote	wracked	**which**	whisper	calf
wrong	writhing	**hour**	whisker	calves
wrist	wrinkle	**while**	rhubarb	halves
wring	wriggle	**nowhere**	wheezy	yolk
wren	wrapping	**whether**	ghastly	folk
wrack	wrestle	rhyme	exhaust	folklore
15 words so far	wrangle	rhythm	whisking	calming
	playwright	vehicle	exhibit	almond
	wriggling	wheel	exhibition	salmon
	wrestling	whisk	rhinoceros	becalm
	34 words so far	53 words so far	72 words so far	91 words so far

	up to 39 Sparking	40–49 Glowing	50–59 Burning	60–69 Sizzling	70+ Red hot!
Score/Date					
Score/Date					

One Minute Wonders

Read the story then draw the picture.

White Whale whizzed towards the wreck. Where had it come from? When had it sunk? Was he too late to help? Luckily, the whole crew were safe and sound in their lifeboat, wrapped up in cosy blankets.

"Can you pull us to safety?" they called out. "We are exhausted!"

"Of course," he answered happily. "It would be an honour!"

Practise writing.

Build your word power.

Brilliant! You made it to the next stage!

Well done!
ui
oo
Silent Letters
ea
ow
ou
aw
au
oy
oi
ir

Going to the toilet is very difficult as you can't have your skin exposed to the cold for long or you will get frostbite, and you can't stop once you have started walking as it's too dangerous. You must go first thing in the morning. Where do you go? You build an ice wall to shelter from the wind, go very quickly and wipe yourself with a pack of ice! How ghastly! At night you have to wee into a bottle. The whole business is exhausting!

Crook on a Hook

By Rosie

Read the words.

Set 1 (10 words)	Set 2 (15 words)	Set 3 (15 words)	Set 4 (15 words)
look	**good**	football	crooked
crook	**book**	booklet	precook
woolly	**stood**	bookcase	hooking
took	**wood**	woody	woollen
cook	shook	mistook	sooty
foot	hood	lookout	hooded
wooden	woof	withstood	goodness
hook	wool	hoody	overtook
brook	nook	hoodwink	crookedly
soot	rook	booking	cookery
10 words so far	looked	cooking	overlook
	cooked	unhook	understood
	booked	looking	woollier
	hooked	footstool	bookcases
	goodbye	unhooked	misunderstood
	25 words so far	40 words so far	55 words so far

One Minute Wonders

	up to 39 Sparking	40–49 Glowing	50–59 Burning	60–69 Sizzling	70+ Red hot!
Score/Date					
Score/Date					

26

Read the story then draw the picture.

Look! A crook in a red woolly hat took all the freshly baked pizza. But luckily, the clever cook caught hold of the crook's foot with his wooden hook! The cook decided that such a bad man should be put in a brook and covered in soot!

Practise writing.

Build your word power.

Brilliant! You made it to the next stage!

You are almost there. With all the energy you are using, you need to eat many more calories than usual. A man usually eats about 2300 calories a day but here you need to eat at least 6000 calories of food. Half of this is used by your body just to keep warm. You took with you the special food suitable for Antarctic expeditions called pemmican. It is made of fat and protein and contains lots of calories in every bite. It is a particularly cold day so thank goodness for your special woolly hat as 20 per cent of your body heat can be lost through your head.

Well done!
ui
oo
Silent Letters
ea
ow
ou
aw
au
oy
oi
ir

ui

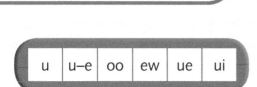

| u | u–e | oo | ew | ue | ui |

Read the words.

Set 1 (7 words)	Set 2 (14 words)	Set 3 (14 words)
juicy	juice	bruising
fruit	sluice	cruises
bruise	juiced	bruises
cruise	cruised	fruitful
suit	bruised	cruising
suitcase	fruits	fruitless
nuisance	swimsuit	fruitier
7 words so far	tracksuit	juicier
	pursuit	fruitiest
	suitor	suitable
	wetsuit	unsuited
	lawsuit	fruitfully
	cruiser	fruitiness
	fruity	unsuitable
	21 words so far	35 words so far

	up to 39 Sparking	40–49 Glowing	50–59 Burning	60–69 Sizzling	70+ Red hot!
Score/Date					
Score/Date					

Read the story then draw the picture.

Poor Juicy Fruit was sad as he had a very nasty bruise.

"We have booked you a cruise to make you feel better," said his friends.

So he found his smart stripy suit and looked for his suitcase but it was nowhere to be seen.

What a nuisance!

Practise writing.

Build your word power.

Brilliant! You've done it!

You feel battered and bruised but you've made it! After 47 gruelling days of pulling your pulk, you have reached the South Pole, one of the planet's last great untouched wildernesses. Your patience, determination and physical and mental strength have been rewarded. You can now add your name to the short list of true adventurers who have made the ultimate journey to the bottom of the world! You have your photograph taken next to the shining globe and celebrate!

Well done!
ui
oo
Silent Letters
ea
ow
ou
aw
au
oy
oi
ir

Sizzling Syllables! ③

Read the syllables.

New *Ski the South Pole* patterns

write	palm	ool	uise	wrong	uice
ook	uit	wrap	half	oot	exhaust

Got it? ☐

Ski the South Pole mix-up

oid	squaw	oof	soy	gow	coun	oud
drea	oist	whole	squir	yolk	bir	aub
fow	eant	calm	hau	ook	uit	thir
wheel	prou	awn	goy	our	stea	auze
poi	uice	uise	spoi	ool	craw	brow
dir	dau	chow	roy	ouge	ood	trea
wrap	ound	ead	brow	raw	oint	cau

Got it? ☐

WordBlaze so far

sau	cen	jois	arves	ead	ture	wrote
sui	ain	ound	nai	ood	guin	gir
turb	tion	troy	cy	awd	ower	eek
cir	ly	ogue	tion	ous	rew	frui
gic	say	ook	cel	auth	eas	age
exhibit	udge	whi	wor	lui	owd	adge
atch	ture	oes	eath	ous	low	ouch
noy	itch	kit	pois	awn	uzz	lue
vir	igh	oose	oat	thir	ooth	eap

Got it? ☐

Fiery Phrases! ③

White Whale	Crook on a Hook	Juicy Fruit

Read the phrases. Do you remember all the spelling patterns you have learnt so far?

Set 1	Set 2	Set 3
what is wrong	looking around	what a nuisance
wrote a letter	where is your hoody	in hot pursuit
wrinkling his nose	the cookery competition	pack your suitcase
wrack your brains	made of beautiful wood	a juicy orange
pull off the wrapper	nook and cranny	a fruitless journey
where are you going	booked the ticket	does this suit me
the ship was wrecked	a football match	you need a wetsuit
which way should we go	you have misunderstood	my tracksuit is dirty
whisked away	by hook or by crook	he felt exploited
while I was waiting	have you understood	such a disloyal friend
the cat's whiskers	I was hoodwinked	pausing for a moment
a whiff of car exhaust	a warm woolly coat	crawling through the bushes
endangered white rhinos	the car overtook	outwitted by the thief
a ghastly mistake	we all said goodbye	cowering in the corner
cut it in half	by the crooked gate	treading carefully
the answer is two	it's on the bookcase	feeling very bruised
talk about the exhibition	a bruised knee	please stop whining
in a while	an unsuitable film	wriggling around
calm down	do you like fruit juice	let's go halves
feel the rhythm	we went on a cruise	landing heavily on the ground
20 phrases	**20 phrases**	**20 phrases**

	up to 29 Sparking	30–39 Glowing	40–49 Burning	50–59 Sizzling	60+ Red hot!
Score/Date					
Score/Date					

Blazing Extras

Read the words.

The Weighty Sheik

ei			
By Carrie			

eight	neighbour	weighed	eighteen
weight	beige	veils	feigning
eighth	sheik	deign	weightless
reign	reins	skein	neighbours
weigh	veins	reigned	weighty
vein	neighs	sleighs	neighbourly
rein	feign	feigned	surveillance
neigh	sheiks	deigned	neighing
veil	freight	eighty	eighteenth

A Great Steak

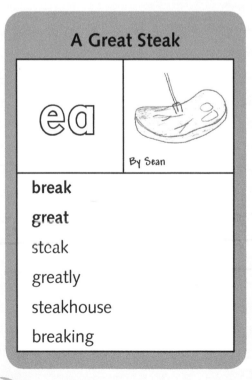

By Sean

break

great

steak

greatly

steakhouse

breaking

The Osprey's Prey

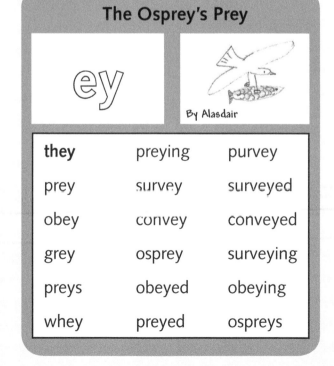

By Alasdair

they	preying	purvey
prey	survey	surveyed
obey	convey	conveyed
grey	osprey	surveying
preys	obeyed	obeying
whey	preyed	ospreys

Youth Group

By Claudia

youth	**wound**	boutique	recoup
group	**mousse**	toucan	goulash
soup	**bouquet**	coupon	boulevard
croutons	**you**	routine	bivouac
route	troupe	cagoule	acoustic
through	coup	subgroup	routinely

The youth group were eating soup with croutons on the route to Oxford when one fell off his bike going through a tunnel and got a horrible wound. They cheered him up with some chocolate mousse and a bouquet of flowers!

Traffic Panic

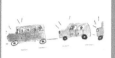

By Siobhan

public	specific
music	republic
traffic	genetic
plastic	Antarctic
topic	electric
magic	dramatic
basic	automatic
panic	academic
logic	democratic
fabric	economic
Arctic	scientific
rhythmic	automatically

I Love Mondays!

◎ **saying short u**
often before v, n and th

By Charlie

love	**brother**	**something**	shove
some	**money**	**another**	honey
other	**above**	**company**	oven
come	**mother**	**otherwise**	wonder
son	**among**	**discover**	shovel
done	**become**	**government**	dozen
none	**cover**	accompany	worry
front	**nothing**	glove	wondered
month	**Monday**	dove	worrying

White Hot Wonder!

Read the words.

Set 1	Set 2	Set 3	Set 4
thirst	poisonous	treading	cookery
crowd	juicy	wreckage	stirring
wriggle	claws	enjoyment	exhausted
taught	growled	misunderstood	thawing
pounce	ahead	sauntering	boisterous
voice	thousands	pursuit	pronounce
joyful	suitable	circulate	glowering
wooden	employ	awkward	voyage
awful	halves	appointment	wheezing
weather	paused	flounce	audition
bruise	hooked	rhythm	unsuitable
suitcase	choice	cowardly	squirming
shouting	sauce	threaten	overtook
allowed	powerful	destroyer	cloudier
exhibition	skirt	sprawled	scrawny
annoying	amount	unconfirmed	however
avoid	jealous	cautious	noisiest
booklet	yawn	checkout	unsteadily
launch	calmly	moisture	overjoyed
breathless	heaviest	powdered	whirled
20 words	20 words	20 words	20 words

Beat your time!

Set 1	Set 2	Sets 1 and 2

Set 3	Set 4	Sets 3 and 4